TRAMS
OF THE ISLE of MAN
1946 ~ present day

STAN BASNETT

Published on the Isle of Man by
Lily Publications, PO Box 33, Ramsey, Isle of Man IM99 4LP
Tel: +44 (0)1624 898446 Fax: +44 (0)1624 898449
E-mail: info@lilypublications.co.uk Web: www.lilypublications.co.uk

Tramways came to the Isle of Man three years after the steam railway, which already had twenty-seven miles of three feet-gauge track linking Douglas to Peel in the west and Port Erin in the south. A retired engineering contractor Thomas Lightfoot came to live in the Isle of Man and purchased a house in Douglas near Little Switzerland. Being of an entrepreneurial nature he soon promoted the idea of a horse tramway along Douglas seafront extending from the harbour to Strathallan Crescent. The year was 1876 and Douglas then was very different to the Douglas of today.

The tramway was built single-track to a gauge of 3ft on the seaward side of the promenade with a number of passing places. The first two trams to arrive were built by Starbuck Car and Wagon Co. Ltd. and were open-top double-deck cars, followed by a single-deck car from the same manufacturer.

The Manx Electric Railway started life as a tramway to serve the Howstrake Estate but soon extended its horizons towards Laxey and became the Douglas and Laxey East Coast Tramway Co. By the end of 1893 a single line had been built as far as Groudle, also to a gauge of 3ft. One year later the line had been doubled and had reached Laxey. The further extension to Ramsey was not completed until 1899. A depot was built on reclaimed land at Port e Vada adjacent to Derby Castle, and

Manx Electric Railway electricity generating station at Port e Vada, Douglas in 1894. (photo Mather & Platt - author's collection)

21st August 1895, the opening day of the Snaefell Mountain Railway at Laxey. (photo MER - author's collection)

additional car sheds followed at Laxey and Ramsey. Electric power was generated initially at Port e Vada in a power station built adjacent to the depot and then supplemented with generating stations at Laxey and Ballaglass.

The first two cars for the tramway were built by George.F.Milnes & Co. Ltd. and they still exist, making them without doubt the oldest working tramcars in the world. The last tramcars acquired in 1906 by the company were built by the United Electric Car Company Ltd. and were the most powerful. At this time the tramway fleet stood at thirty motor cars and twenty nine trailers.

The same promoters formed the Snaefell Mountain Railway and by 1895 had built a tramway to the top of the island's highest mountain. The audacity of these Victorian entrepreneurs can only be marvelled at when viewed from the perspective of the present day. The only mountain such a proposal would face now

would be a mountain of red tape! It would never happen.

However, build it they did but to a gauge of 3ft 6ins in order to accommodate the Fell braking rail and calliper braking gear used on the descent. Double track was laid to the summit with an electricity generating station constructed at the half-way point. Two buildings were constructed, one at the summit and the other where the line crossed the mountain road, the latter becoming known as the Bungalow. There was one intermediate halt at the Bungalow and both buildings served refreshments. The depot, which housed six cars, was located at Laxey. All the passenger cars were built by G.F.Milnes & Co. Ltd. A works car was built by the company and it used bogies from one of the passenger cars as required when used on winter maintenance.

In 1896 the same local dignitaries flushed with the success of their other tramway ventures

This is one of the cable diverter pulleys in the diverter pit under York Road opposite Waverley Court. It is one of the few remaining traces of the Douglas Cable Tramway.

acquired the Douglas Horse Tramway and looked at ways of extending their tram network through the town. They faced opposition to the electrification of the promenade tramway and so then looked at extending into upper Douglas. Cable traction was seen as the only way to tackle the steep gradients as their proposal encircled what was then seen as the future extent of Douglas.

The Upper Douglas Cable Tramway was eventually constructed as a 3ft gauge cable-operated tramway serving upper Douglas from Victoria Street to York Road with an extension to Broadway where the line had a physical link to the horse tramway. The line was complete and operational by 1896 and lasted until 1929. There were fifteen cars, all but two of which were built by Milnes & Co. The exceptions were cable cars No.69 and No.70 which were built by the United Electric Car Co. The cars were housed in a purpose-built

depot and engine house built just below the highest point of the line at York Road.

Now nothing remains to indicate that it ever existed. A sheltered housing complex has now replaced the depot, which had been used as a bus depot after the cable tramway closed. As far as I know the diverter pulleys for the cable from the engine house still remain in a pit under the roadway and as you will see other remnants were discovered in the course of road improvement works, but by far the most interesting find was two almost intact cars being used as a private residence which have since been restored as one car – a lasting tribute to the system.

In 1900 the bubble burst. It appeared that funds from Dumbell's Bank, the directors of which were inexorably linked to the tramway ventures, had been misappropriated to fund the schemes. When the Bank failed the day became known as 'Black Saturday'; many local people and firms lost money, including my grandfather Cannell. The tramway undertakings went into liquidation and the east coast tramways emerged in 1901 as the Manx Electric Railway Company. The horse tramway and cable tramway were taken over by the Douglas Corporation.

All of this is well covered in detail in Keith Pearson's definitive history 'Isle of Man Tramways' and the late Connery Chappell's book 'The Dumbell Affair', publications with which I was proud to be associated. The latter author I have to thank for his encouragement in any aspirations I had towards writing – oh, and also for introducing me to the delights of pink gin!

A fire at Laxey depot in 1930 destroyed a number of motor cars and trailers which were not replaced. The Manx Electric Railway suffered a further setback later in the same year when a freak cloudburst caused flooding in the area of Laxey. It inundated their power plant at Laxey and due to a problem with their automatic weir damaged Glen

Road and flooded properties for which they were held responsible. By 1934 the company ceased generating their own electricity and purchased power from the Isle of Man Electricity Board.

The company never really recovered from these setbacks but struggled on and just about survived until after the Second World War, but the lack of money spent on maintenance was now beginning to take its toll on the infrastructure. Most of the track needed replacing and the overhead was in desperate need of new poles – corrosion from salt-laden air being a major problem. Nonetheless it remained as a private company until 1957 when it was purchased by the Isle of Man Government and continues as a nationalised entity.

The Snaefell Mountain Railway became nationalised in 1957 as part of the acquisition of the Manx Electric Railway. It survives to the present day despite a move early in its Government ownership for the track to be removed and for it to become a road to the summit.

In 1896 another tramway was promoted south from Douglas and built, uniquely for the island, to the standard gauge of 4ft 8½ins. The company was styled as the Douglas Southern Electric Tramways Ltd. Its route was spectacular as it clung to the cliff edge throughout its length and spanned three inlets at Pigeon Stream, Horseleap and Wallberry on lattice girder bridges. Most tramways in passing through their legislative process have to prove a need and a purpose. In this case the single-line track with passing places went from Douglas to a point in the middle of nowhere at Keristal almost three miles from its terminus on Douglas Head. It eventually served a Victorian pleasure resort at Port Soderick by means of a cliff lift.

The company had a power generating station at Pigeon Stream and a depot at Little Ness, a remote headland, which must have been one of the most exposed tram depots anywhere, housing eight motor cars and eight trailers. The line never re-opened after the Second World War but its demolition and formation into a scenic roadway just fall within the remit of the period covered by this book. One tramcar exists in preservation and is presently at the Tramway Museum at Crich.

The surviving tramways have enjoyed a renaissance in recent years, much of the track has been re-laid and some of the old buildings have been replaced. There is still much to do but they have survived for our enjoyment and to give the visitor to the island a unique experience of a Victorian transport system. So here now is the story of these tramways over the last fifty years told in pictures, all of which were taken by me except where otherwise known or acknowledged. Some were taken in my teens and are of dubious quality; nonetheless I hope you enjoy them.

Stan Basnett
Glen Vine

A winter photograph from the 1960s of MER tramcar *No.1* on track maintenance duty at the Dhoon.

The view enjoyed by thousands of visitors to the island in the period under review. The only difference between 1965 and now is that there are now in 2008 sixty thousand cars registered on the island as opposed to a little over nine thousand then. Oh, and more than a little regeneration of the Victorian facade of Queens Promenade.

Horse-car *No.45* dating from 1908 and built by G.C.Milnes, Voss & Co. Ltd. is lightly loaded on a rather miserable summer's day – even Freddy Callister the driver is well wrapped up against the elements. However, the horse seems to be enjoying the run past Palace Terrace.

At the start of every season horses that had been out to pasture all winter at various locations on the island had to get back into harness and get used once again to pulling a tram. The horses weren't always very happy to start work having enjoyed a winter of freedom. Here a horse is out very early in the season before the visitors have arrived, undergoing familiarisation under the watchful eye of the stable foreman Jimmy Moughtin, Councillor (later Alderman) E. Griffin Chairman of the Tramway Committee at the horse's head and driver Tommy Maddrell.

Horse-car **No 31** is running on the wrong track while other employees are cleaning out the grooved tram-track on the other line.

The Douglas Corporation always had some form of mechanical sweeper available to clean up the horse-droppings from the promenade, although their normal duty was street cleaning. The cost of cleaning up after the trams has become more of a contentious issue in recent years and is becoming a cost burden on the operation of the trams.

All horses used on the tramway have to be trained to pull the tram and respond to unfamiliar sounds. Problems were usually confined to young horses or newly acquired horses, in which case an experienced horse would be harnessed along with the novice to a double swingle attached to the tram and run alongside the experienced horse. Immediately after the Second World War, as soon as the internment camp fences had been removed, horse-cars ran a winter service due to the scarcity of buses. Double-deck trams were used on occasion and employed two horses if there was a strong wind.

This is the interior of horse-car *No.18* which was originally a double-deck tram purchased second-hand from South Shields in 1887, before the tramway was acquired by the Douglas Corporation. It was converted by the Corporation in 1906 to a single deck car. Note the beautiful roof construction. It still exists and was converted back to a double-deck tram in 1989.

Horse-car **No.1**, the second to carry this number, dates from 1913. It was built by G.C.Milnes, Voss & Co. Ltd. and was one of the last built by that company. Photographed on Loch Promenade with a full load you can see here the traces are slack and the horse is having to trot to keep ahead of the car. All cars have modern roller bearings fitted and run very freely. The skill of the driver is important to stop the horse being caught by the tram.

Find a wet day in summer and you can still ride on one of these cars and enjoy a flashback in time. Car **No.18** leads a trio of horse-cars and still in its single-deck form. Remember it was converted from a double-deck car to single-deck in 1906. It now survives as a double-deck car once again having been converted back in 1989.

Horse-car **No.27** was purchased by Isle of Man Tramways in 1892 from G.F.Milnes & Co. Ltd. Together with **No.s 28** and **29** they became known as the "Pullman" cars. They represented the very pinnacle of tramcar design and have many features which can be seen on some of the early electric cars of the Manx Electric Railway.

No. 18 again just about to be pushed into the Derby Castle depot at the end of Strathallan Crescent with the horse no doubt finished for the day and judging by its ears - knows it!

It is unusual for an easterly gale to strike in summer. When it did, before the extension of the breakwater, and it coincided with a high tide, you could guarantee that chaos ensued. This is what happened in September 1967 during such a storm. Horse-cars became derailed, the horses found it difficult to keep their footing on the stones and seaweed that had washed up on the promenade and buses had to try and pass them on the wrong side of the road. The fear in this situation is that a horse could shy and bolt which had of course happened in the past.

Here it's "all hands to" to try and re-rail car **No.46** with the stable foreman holding the horse and being supervised by Horse-car Inspector Jack Dugdale who no doubt had seen it all before. The car was eventually re-railed and the horse then put on the opposite end to move the car back towards the Casino so that traffic could clear Broadway junction and allow the track to be cleared. The loss of many of the intermediate cross-overs restricted the options and aggravated the situation.

Above: The livestock carrier *Colebrooke* of the Belfast Steamship Co. Ltd. arrived at Douglas at a quarter past one in the morning on 22nd April 1966 with twenty-four horses from Northern Ireland for Douglas Corporation. They were discharged, assembled in groups and walked from the Battery Pier to the stables at the bottom of Summerhill. Imagine trying to do that now!

Right: The start of a day's work for one of the horses as it is walked down to the depot from the stables. Horses are changed after their normal run in service at the bottom of Summerhill opposite the stables.

Whenever a horse-car became due for either repainting or repair it would be taken to York Road depot towed by Douglas Corporation AEC Regent III *No.60* which had a tow bar fitted for the specific purpose. The tram would be loaded onto a special dolly fitted with rails at Derby Castle and travel along the Promenade and up Broadway, turning into Waverley Terrace and the back of the York Road bus depot.

Why, do I hear you ask? Well, the reason was historic. The Corporation eventually owned the Upper Douglas Cable Tramway including the depot and engine house which were located on York Road. The cable tramway had a connection with the horse tramway at Broadway and because the coach builders and painters all worked at York Road Depot it was logical to take trams to York Road for servicing and repair, a cable tram being used to tow trams up Broadway to the depot. Yes old habits die hard but in fairness all of the maintenance staff were still at York Road when it became the bus depot. Later when the stables had a Land Rover that was used to tow the trams to the depot.

In 1976 the horse tramway celebrated its Centenary in great style. These next photographs illustrate a little of what went on behind the scenes to prepare for the event. York Road paint shop housed in the old cable car engine house was packed to the gunwales with horse-cars being repainted and prepared for the event.

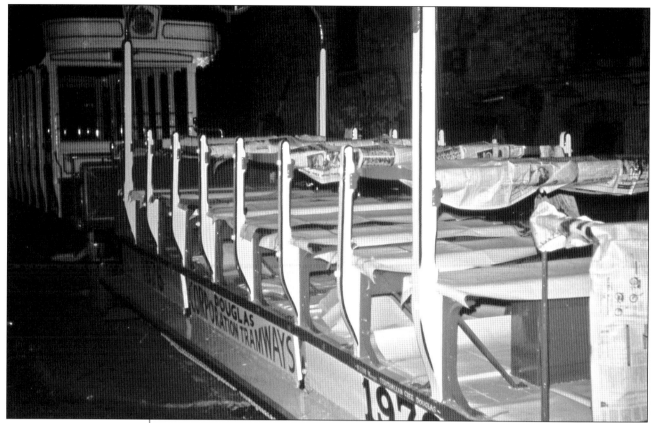

One of the horse-cars which was being refurbished for the Centenary celebrations was "toastrack" car *No.12*. It was purchased in 1888 from G.F. Milnes & Co. Ltd. as one of four eight-bench open cars. Its lamp boxes and supporting arches were removed after the Second World War after the cars had been stored in a yard at the bottom of Summerhill. It was these characteristic arches that gave them the name "toastrack" and *No.12* had its replaced for the Centenary. Only three remain in service as car *No.11* is in store at Homefield, the former bus depot of IOM Road Services.

Double-deck horse-car *No.14* was one of six double-deck horse-cars acquired from South Shields in 1887. Originally *No.13* it was re-numbered after the original *No.14* was damaged at the depot by a rock fall. In 1955 it left the island to become an exhibit at the Museum of British Transport at Clapham. It came back to the island for the Centenary, was re-furbished and was used for the opening ceremony on Centenary day. It ran on special occasions until 1991 when it was transferred to the Manx Museum to become a permanent exhibit.

DOUGLAS ISLE OF MAN

DOUGLAS CORPORATION TRAMWAYS

14

Here is car **No.14**, its repaint completed, being removed from the paint shop at York Road and prepared for removal to Derby Castle depot. The origin of the paint shop as the engine room of the cable tramway is clearly seen from the front elevation.

Now things were beginning to happen and it was hard to hide the fact that the Centenary was going to be a big occasion. The re-furbished cars were being brought back to the depot at Derby Castle behind the faithful AEC in July 1976. Short "toastrack" *No.12*, now restored almost to original condition, is being returned to the depot.

Car *No.12* is being manhandled onto the depot fan having just arrived from York Road behind the AEC.

Car **No.29**, arrives at Derby Castle to be off-loaded onto the depot fan and placed on the traverser before being cleaned for the Centenary parade. In the background is the restored cable car of which more later.

Early in the morning of 9th August 1976 this was the scene at Strathallan Crescent as the AEC Regent III took four horse-cars to the Sea Terminal in preparation for the Centenary celebrations. It was the first of four runs, the last involving seven horse-cars behind DC1 *No.60*. Altogether twenty horse-cars and the restored cable car were assembled at the Sea Terminal for the grand Centenary procession.

With all the horse-cars assembled at the Sea Terminal, on the otherwise little used double track leading to the tram shelter, fifty horses suitably prepared and carrying their name tags on their harnesses were paraded along the promenade by their crews, splendidly turned out in new uniforms for the occasion. The promenade was lined on both sides with more people than would normally come to see a carnival.

Double-deck car **No.14** gets the celebrations under way. it was driven by the guest of honour for the occasion Miss Ann Moore who was ably supervised by Stevie Stricket, now the stable foreman and an old friend from my cycling days.

The horse-cars being located on the promenade were often used for charity events and publicity stunts. These two photographs clearly illustrate the sort of thing that went on. The top photograph shows Jimmy Saville pulling a horse-car along Douglas Promenade - and yes he went the whole length of the promenade, harness and all, with the Mayor of Douglas driving! The lower photograph shows an entourage of young boys chasing car **No.44** with Sean Connery (James Bond) on board. The two professional photographers standing behind the driver recording the event are John Gaggs and the late Bill Peters, two very good friends. The police outrider behind the tram is my brother-in-law - "bodyguard to James Bond" would look good on a CV!

Car *No.39* (above) was one of three acquired in 1902 by the Douglas Corporation, who were by then the owners of the horse tramway, from G.F.Milnes & Co. Ltd., almost the last to be made by that company. They were thirty-two-seat eight-bench cars. The photograph (below) taken on Loch Promenade opposite Granville Street shows car *No.29* passing roofed "toastrack" car *No.47* supplied by G.C.Milnes, Voss & Co. Ltd. in 1911 and is included to show the normal manner in which prams were carried slung over the brake handle. This tram currently is out of service and in store at Homefield garage.

Car **No.48** was one of three supplied by Vulcan Motor and Engineering Co. Ltd. of Southport in 1935 to a design by Mr. C.F. Wolsey, the Corporation Transport Manager. They were convertible all-weather cars with folding sides seating 34 as open cars and 27 when operating closed. It and **No.50** were broken up in 1982 but **No.49** survives and is store also at Homefield destined for preservation.

Two "toastracks" passing on Loch Promenade. Car **No.21** dates from 1890 and was lengthened in 1936 to become a forty-seat car. The top boards fitted later to the "toastracks" carried advertising for the Villa Marina which was changed every Monday.

The presence and novelty of the horse-cars on the promenade at Douglas made them the focus of attention. This was an opportunity not missed by the Corporation who were keen to sell advertising space not only for events at the Villa Marina but at Onchan Stadium and Palace and Derby Castle venues. Several trams have been used from time to time for exclusive advertising for events such as the TT and the Casino.

A sunny summer day to end on for the review of the horse tramway as horse-car **No.34** arrives at Derby Castle and visitors join the next electric tramcar to Laxey. I hope that the horse trams, so much a part of the Douglas scene, last into the future. The pressures of modern traffic seem more than ever to threaten their existence.

Douglas had a cable tramway serving Upper Douglas from 1896 to 1929 and it was built to a gauge of 3ft. Now in 2008 nothing remains as tangible evidence that it ever existed except for one tram which we have seen lurking in the background of photographs of the horse tram Centenary celebrations. The trams were sold in 1929 to Chas. Mc. Carten and he intended to sell them on as summer holiday homes. Two did eventually become the permanent home for the Keig family at the Killane at Jurby. Here they are, **No.72** and **No.73** where they survived until 1968 before being retrieved by enthusiasts and one car assembled from the remaining parts.

In the Introduction a photograph shows all that could be seen in the diverter pit at York Road of one of the cable pulleys. We all assumed that it was the only pulley surviving but during the course of roadworks in the 1990s two more were uncovered at Stanley Mount in Broadway and at Victoria Street sitting, in their pits having been covered over and buried by subsequent road surfacing. The photographs on this page show the pulley retrieved from the Victoria Street terminus. I think what impressed me most was the size of the wheel which hopefully will be incorporated into the future Museum of Transport.

I was among those led by the late Keith Pearson, the driving force in the cable car restoration, who got their hands dirty. Yes, it is me under that mop of 70s hair working on one of the bogies at Derby Castle depot in the rush to get the cable car running on its wheels on the horse tramway track for the Centenary. *(photo: Gillian Basnett.)*

And here is the finished article with its two numbers, different at each end, indicating its pedigree on Centenary Day ready to be pulled along the promenade by a Land Rover loaned by Messrs Mylchreests, the local agent. The cable car is now capable of ingeniously running on its own. It too will become part of the new Museum of Transport.

The Douglas Southern
Electric Tramway power
station at Pigeon Stream in
the process of demolition
and the adjacent bridge which
was demolished by Highway
Board employees using
explosive charges.

The Douglas Southern Electric Tramway or as it was colloquially known the Marine Drive Tramway existed from 1896 to 1940 after which the tramway ran no more. It remained intact until 1946 at which time the drive and all remaining trams and track were purchased by the IOM Highway and Transport Board for the IOM Government. The objcct was to create a scenic roadway from Douglas to Port Soderick which wasn't completed until 1963. The first thing that the Highway Board had to do was remove the tramway and demolish three major bridges which were considered unsafe. The first was at Pigeon Stream and is illustrated on this and the preceding page. The only surviving tram is not on the island but is preserved at Crich Tramway Museum in Derbyshire. Some signs of the trackbed can, however, still be seen on the Marine Drive if you know where to look.

Another now defunct tramway but which was in use during the period covered by this book was the Ramsey Queens Pier Tramway. Built to the 3ft gauge it ran for a length of 2,300ft. The full complement of stock can be seen in this photograph In 1970. the Hibberd "planet" locomotive, tramcar and luggage trolley with the Wickham railcar in the distance.

This Wadsworth cliff lift serviced the Falcon Cliff Hotel which is now converted to offices but in the 1960s and 70s it was one of the places to go in the summer with its dance hall commanding a superb view over Douglas Bay, rivalling the Douglas Bay Hotel and its Texas Bar and the Douglas Head Hotel. All now a past memory.

A 1970s view of Derby Castle terminus with the elaborate horse-car shelter still in place. Plenty of trams about but a miserable day and the closed saloons are in evidence but not many visitors.

Car *No.19* dating from 1899 was one of four bought by the IOM Tramways & Electric Power Co., forerunners of the Manx Electric Railway Co., as winter saloons. It is seen here on an evening Groudle service negotiating Port Jack road crossing.

Car **No.2** and its sister car **No.1** were purchased in 1893 by the original Howstrake estate tramway in 1893 and they still exist. It seems like sacrilege now but in the 50s and 60s they were used in the winter as works cars - simply because they were the oldest cars in the fleet. Here the overhead gang are at work in the Derby Castle depot.

"Paddle box" car **No.16** dating from 1898 was built by G.F.Milnes & Co. Ltd. as an open American-style open cross-bench car. Here it is receiving attention to its trolley in the depot at Derby Castle and the date is 1963

The old timber-framed tram shed at Derby Castle served the MER well until the whole depot was modernised in the early 1990s.

Tunnel car **No.5** was another G.F. Milnes & Co. Ltd. tram-car supplied as one of six ordered by the tramway company in 1894. Two were lost in the disastrous fire at the tram shed at Laxey and only **No. 7** and **No.9** remain in near original condition internally with longitudinal seating. **No.5** and **No.6** were fitted with flip-over seating across the car and a central partition.

Lewis Gale not long after his promotion to shed foreman at Derby Castle photographed in the workshop at Derby Castle which was formerly the electric power station. I had been at school with his son Peter which helped access to otherwise forbidden places!

Laxey tram shed was rebuilt after the fire in 1930 but even when this photograph was taken in 1969 it was in a parlous state notwithstanding the fact that it was in Government ownership. Car **No's.1** and **2** spent much of their time here, still being used as works cars in the winter and only pressed into service at peak times in the summer. **No.1** had a wood-framed windscreen fitted to provide some winter protection for the driver, **No.2** still remained the "wire car". No one really appreciated the rarity of these trams which are now fully refurbished and remain the oldest working trams in public service in the world.

Here are two more photographs of **No.2** at work with the "wire gang" carrying out maintenance work on the overhead behind Waterloo Road in Ramsey (above) and at Lag Birragh on the King Edward Road, Onchan (below).

Car **No.1** at Port Jack and employees of the MER carrying out track repair following problems with the track moving out of gauge (see page 47).

A final view of car **No.2** with one of the two tower wagons in use at that time. The MER staff were all old hands and well used to improvisation which was just as well because spares for the overhead were almost unobtainable then. Poles were also in a poor state and despite Government ownership funding for replacements was tight.

Car *No.16* being "warmed up" at Derby Castle after being in store all winter and out of use. The sea air was not conducive to keeping the motors in good condition so the brakes would be screwed down hard and the controller put on one notch to dry out the insulation! The date it started is on the dash in chalk and the photograph was taken on 11th April 1963.

This is a later view of car **No.1** at work showing the dodger fitted to the driving ends for driver protection. The track is being maintained at Ballure.

The MER staff were resourceful and could carry out almost anything that came their way. In this photograph the Derby Castle has been demolished and work is starting on Summerland but a south-easterly gale has wreaked havoc with the track which would have to be repaired before double-track working could resume.

Here are the engineering department with the remedial work well in hand. Two cars have been pressed into action car, *No.9* with a "Dreadnought" flatbed fabricated from one of the disused trailer cars. Another unidentified car has more ballast in one of the six-ton goods wagons.

This section of track at Derby Castle suffered during the construction of the Summerland entertainment centre and when the building work was completed the opportunity was taken to re-lay the track completely. One of the "tunnel cars" is on works duty sporting the awful single windscreen which totally spoiled the character of the car.

Car **No.26** and car **No.27** are very interesting tram cars: both were delivered from Milnes of Birkenhead in 1898 and entered the fleet as trailer cars. They were motorised in 1903 along with two other cars from the same batch. Their footboards had to be cutaway and stepped to accommodate the motorised trucks and subsequently became known as the "paddleboxes"; and carried new numbers as part of the motor fleet along with car **No.16**. **No.26** (above) is passing Derby Castle theatre at the depot entrance in August 1963. As a St. John Ambulance Brigade cadet I did first aid duty at Derby Castle between 1949 and 1953 and my entry was through the anonymous brown door behind the tram - the stage door. It isn't surprising really that I became more interested in the trams. **No.27** (below) is photographed at Port Jack passing the Moo Kow ice cream parlour with a Groudle night service tram in July 1964. The MER has always employed extra summer staff and students vied for the jobs on offer.

Here is a photograph of tunnel car **No.7** approaching Derby Castle terminus in the summer of 1961. Derby Castle Hotel, Theatre and Ballroom are all still there. Does it bring back memories?

The depot at Derby Castle on a miserable September day also in 1961 with winter saloon **No.21** and car **No.2** back on winter duty as the "wire car".

45

I mentioned Lewis Gale earlier and he was good to keep me informed about what was going on. Here is one of the unusual sights which occurred from time to time at the beginning of winter. Snaefell cars needing attention to bodywork would be taken off their 3ft 6ins. bogies at Laxey and transferred to spare 3ft. bogies kept for the purpose. The overhead collectors would also be removed and the cars brought into Derby Castle for the work to be carried out in the paint shop. On this occasion, which was 30th November 1964, car **No.5** was used to take Snaefell car **No.1** into Douglas - they even stopped for a photo shot at Baldromma!

The condition of the track has been mentioned earlier and its deteriorating condition meant that derailments were all too frequent. Here car **No.20** is off the road at Groudle Holiday Camp (remember that?). The solution was to invite the Territorial Army to carry out a full scale engineering exercise to re-lay the track from Far End to this corner. I told you in "THE AILSA YEARS" that the MER were resourceful - even in Government ownership!

Car **No.s 14** & **15** were acquired from G.F.Milnes & Co. Ltd. in 1898 along with car **No.16** and car **No.18**. These cross-bench cars had glazed bulkheads and a clerestory roof and were later fitted with pull down roller shutters. **No.16** of the quartet was fitted with different motor bogies in 1903 and became a "paddlebox": compare this photograph with that on page 41. Both cars are currently out of service and at Homefield in store.

When the MER ceased generating their own electricity and took their supply from the island's grid they had to convert the AC supply to DC and reduce the voltage. Conversion to DC was done by using mercury arc rectifiers such as this one which was located at Groudle. These have been gradually replaced with more modern equipment.

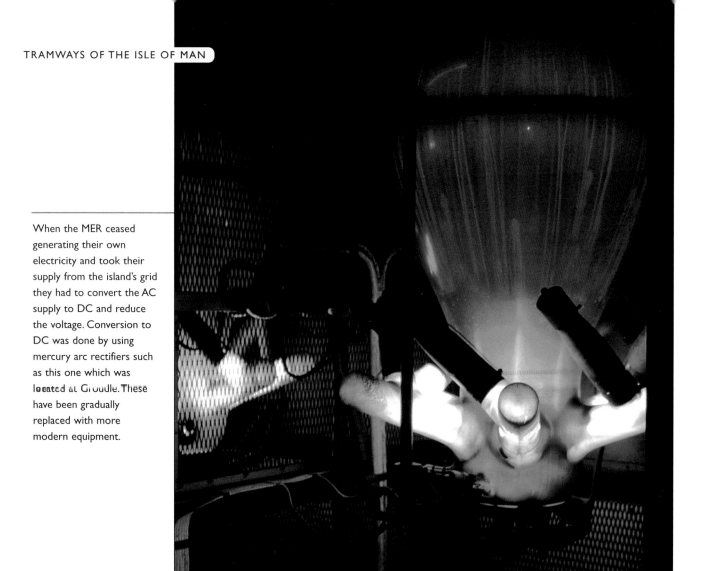

The Centenary celebrations of the Snaefell Mountain Railway included running Isle of Man Railway **No.15 Caledonia** to the summit of Snaefell. Trials took place in wintry conditions during the winter of 1994/95.

MER "tunnel car" *No.5* crossing Groudle Bridge, a wonderful stone-built bridge with graceful high arches only appreciated from below.

The celebrations for the MER Centenary in 1993 started three years before the event. A press photographic publicity event was staged at Laxey late in 1991. It was to give a foretaste of what was to come with some unforgettable run-pasts for the press photographers.

A number of trials took place early in 1995 with IMR **No.15 Caledonia** in preparation for the Snaefell Mountain Railway Centenary and it is photographed on the mountain section of the Snaefell Mountain Railway between Bungalow and the Summit to satisfy the Railway Inspector that braking arrangements were satisfactory, giving the opportunity to see something that is hardly likely to happen ever again.

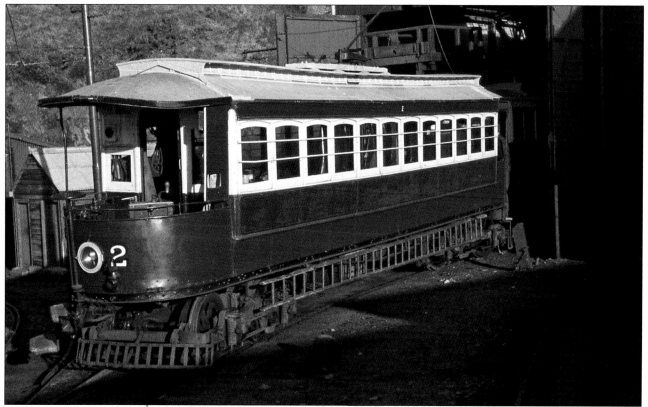

Another photograph of MER car **No.2** taken on 30th November 1962, this time in colour at Derby Castle depot with the tower wagon.

Car **No.2** with the tower wagon and the "wire gang" working on the overhead catenary at Lag Birragh, the bend above Far End (the name of the last house on King Edward Road) on 22nd March 1963 with my trusty motorbike parked precariously against the fence! Little did I know how well I was to get to know these men three years later.

Daryl Gribbin and George Lawson, two very good friends and long-serving employees on both systems of the tramway network looking immaculate for the centenary celebrations.

Not the sort of picture that the Tourist Board welcomed, but rainy summer days were brilliant for visiting enthusiasts and locals to experience riding in the saloon horse-cars and the winter saloons on the MER.

A colour photograph taken approaching Baldromma Crossing of car **No.5** driven by Lewis Gale taking Snaefell car **No.1** to Douglas as described earlier.

Isle of Man Post issued a set of stamps to commemorate the Centenary of the Snaefell Mountain Railway and the Splendour of Steam on 8th February 1995 with a spectacular launch employing just about every mode of transport. The first day covers were taken to the summit in one of the Civil Aviation Authority vehicles to be franked legitimately at the summit. This vehicle was used between the Bungalow and the summit by CAA employees to access their transmitter because the overhead is taken down over the top section in winter to avoid wind and ice damage.

Snaefell car **No.5** descends into Laxey Station from the depot with the tower wagon to carry out maintenance on the overhead in the station area. The photograph shows the car in original condition with the knifeboard advertising panel on the roof, long before its rebuild following its almost total destruction

"Tunnel car" *No.9* (above) of the Manx Electric Railway fitted with the snow plough which was used to keep the tramway open by continually running during periods of snowfall. The result of this effort was best illustrated during the winter of 1964/65 when the east coast tramway remained the only link with Ramsey for several days until the roads were cleared. Whitebridge hadn't been cleared and Baldromma was as far as anyone could reach with a vehicle on the morning of 4th March 1965. MER car *No.22* (below) passes with ease with a full complement of warm passengers!

A number of different colour schemes have been applied to Manx Electric Railway cars over the period under review, usually, but not always, associated with celebrating significant events in the tramway's history. They have always been publicity-conscious and have used some of the many liveries carried at different periods to good effect. MER car **No.21** appeared in the 1899 livery that the winter saloons carried when new, and is seen at Ballure.

Here MER car **No.2**, now no longer neglected and recognised for its historical significance, is carrying an unusual purple lake livery and looking truly magnificent.

Derby Castle was still in full operation when this photograph was taken in the late afternoon when all the visitors were returning from Ramsey and Laxey in time for their boarding house dinners. Trailers would be hand-shunted past the cross-over and taken back to the depot.

Car *No.19* at Bulgham passing the site of the retaining wall which collapsed the following year, seriously damaging the stability of the tramway and threatened the highway.

The island had one of its rare heavy snowfalls in the winter of 1964/65 which severely disrupted the steam railway and bus services but the MER managed to keep one line open during the snowstorm by continually running trams between Douglas and Ramsey. On 4th March 1965 this was the scene at Baldromma with winter saloon *No.22* passing a GPO telephone engineers' van stuck while trying to get to Laxey. Whitebridge Hill at this time was still impassable. One up for the MER!

A general view of Laxey in the height of summer traffic in 1969.

Following a call for assistance from the Manx Electric Railway Board, surveyors from the IOM Highway Board went to Bulgham on 17th November 1966 to examine a wall which the MER had been keeping under observation and where they had detected recent movement. Before a second opinion could be given as to how to relieve the obvious water pressure building behind the wall it partly collapsed on 21st January followed, a week later by a complete collapse.

The collapse was largely confined to the outer skin of the masonry retaining structure, ingeniously constructed using random vertical coursing which had allowed vertical settlement to occur without affecting its strength. It could not,however, resist the outward pressure of a build-up of water behind the wall with the inevitable result. The deformation of the seaward track can be seen in this photograph. It was no longer safe to run trams over the section and the overhead had to be cut and fed from different feeders. Here work is in progress.

The problem was exacerbated by the fact that both of the tower wagons were Laxey side of the failure. One tower wagon was moved to the other side by securing a rope to it, then around a pole on the other side and a tram used to pull it over the failed section. Work could then proceed on the overhead alterations on both sides of the collapse. Some stock was moved in the same manner.

Throughout the whole of this time observations were kept on the stability of the road and the tram trackbed by Highway Board surveyors. Meanwhile Fondedile Foundations Ltd. were engaged as specialist contractors using a pali-radice patent piling system to effect the repair. Core drilling using rotary non-percussive drills commenced followed by pouring, in situ, a criss-cross of reinforced concrete piles. The work was satisfactorily carried out without a single hard hat or reflective jacket in sight!

After the piles had been poured they were topped with a cantilevered reinforced concrete deck (left) on which the rails would be re-laid and ballasted. While the work was in progress a temporary platform and spur were created at both ends to allow service cars for Ramsey to continue to operate the service - passengers walking on the roadway between the two stops.

The lack of water supply at the construction site for the cement slurry was initially a problem for the contractor but the MER, resourceful as ever, came up with a solution utilising an old tank from a fuel delivery vehicle and mounting it on one of the "Dreadnoughts", filling it at the Dhoon as required. I said that I would get to know the "line gang" better and so I did as George Collister set about cutting my hair one lunch time in car *No.2* which we used as our mess hut! Although these photographs were taken in March 1967 and we still had the road under daily observation for settlement, we were still there in May as the job drew to a close in time for the summer traffic.

In March 1964 I was involved in the survey of the cliff face at Bulgham to determine its stability prior to scaling taking place. It was ideal for a chap like me; I could watch the trams go by and work at the same time! Car *No. 21* passes car *No. 20* still on winter service. Little did I know that I would be back in less than two years, time and spend a whole winter here.

69

Here is another shot of a winter saloon off the track in the section between Port Jack and Groudle which gave such a lot of trouble before the Territorial Army got to work. The phenomenon has continued on and off since with heat expansion of the rails being one of the problems.

Anything but heat is the problem here as everyone is called out to clear snow and free the points at the Groudle cross-over. Car *No.7* is ready to change tracks and return to Derby Castle.

"Tunnel car" **No.6** rounds the curve approaching Ballellin (above) in September 1993 and "paddlebox" car **No.26** (below) is just leaving Groudle in the midday sun on 1st June 1963.

There is no doubt about the effort that the MER staff put into the preparations for the Centenary celebrations. Car *No.22* pauses at Baldrine Halt resplendent in new livery and gleaming varnish.

Car *No.6* again as it passes Ballafayle, Maughold. It was repainted and overhauled for the Centenary celebrations in 1993. At the same time the square end windows which had been installed in 1978 to improve driver visibility were removed and the twin windows and centre mullion frame reinstated, after which it looked like a proper trams again.

The two photographs on this page are included as a tribute to the unfailing enthusiasm of Keith Pearson, who sadly passed away in 2008, for the Manx Electric Railway. In the photograph on the left taken in April 1966 he is seen with Mr. Watson and Roy Cannell at one of the overhead feeders on King Edward Road asking questions in infinite detail for his book Isle of Man Tramways which became the definitive history of all the systems.

Keith Pearson (on the right) on one of his last visits to the island is seen at the Centenary celebrations with Maurice Faragher, long-time servant of the MER and later National Transport.

In 1894 George F. Milnes of Birkenhead supplied six cars to the Snaefell Mountain Railway. They remained basically unchanged until 1975 when problems with ageing electrical gear initiated dramatic changes to the fleet. Car *No.2* (above) seen in 1963 starting the climb out of Laxey with Brown's Cafe in the background when it was still Brown's Cafe. Car *No.1* (below) is braking hard as it approaches Laxey Station and on the original transparency you can see the sparks flying off the centre Fell braking rail!

Car Nos. **3** and **4** in Laxey Station in August 1963 ready for the start of the day and showing the contrast between the original SMR livery and the dreadful "institution" green and white livery adopted on nationalisation. **No.4** held the dubious honour of being the last car to carry the colour scheme lasting until 1975. The Milnes lineage of these cars can be compared to MER "tunnel cars" on which they were based although wider. The "tunnel cars" also had the barred windows when new. The Snaefell shed foreman Allan McMullen is in the photograph.

Car **No.1** in Laxey Station waits for the next full load of passengers from Douglas - August 1965. The photograph shows the roof-mounted advertising knifeboard on the clerestory roof to good effect.

This is the view (above) inside the original depot at Laxey which housed the Snaefell cars and where much of the maintenance was carried out under Allan McMullen's supervision - he was an excellent engineer. Keen observation will note the fully air-conditioned shed! Car **No.5** was to suffer a disastrous fire in August 1970 when it was totally destroyed at the summit. Contrast the old shed with the new (right) as car **No.3** sits fully re-painted waiting for its bow collectors to be fitted and the Centenary celebrations to begin.

Above: Another flash from the past during the 1963 TT. Car *Nos 2,3,4* and *5* (left to right) sit below the Bungalow running a shuttle service to the Bungalow from Laxey - something still popular today with race enthusiasts. *No.6* and *No.1* were the other side of the TT course running a reduced service to the summit. Below: Car *No.2* climbs the mountain and has just passed car *No.1* on the descent above Lhergy Veg. The line climbs along the south side of the glacial valley above Laxey, giving the passenger dramatic views over Agneash and the derelict Snaefell lead mines.

By the mid-1970s the condition of the motors on these trams had deteriorated to such an extent that the whole question of their future hung in the balance. Rescue came from London Transport who provided new motors and trucks which were gradually fitted to all cars. At the same time wear on the centre braking rail led to the fitting of rheostatic braking to the cars from 1976 utilising redundant equipment from a number of trams withdrawn from service in Aachen in Germany. All the photographs of cars on this page show the roof-mounted resistors associated with the electrical braking. Car *No.5* (above) in its rebuilt condition, without a clerestory light, following the fire is passing the site of the original generating station for the line just below the Bungalow. Car *Nos.1 & 4* (below) sit patiently in Laxey Station waiting for passengers.

The two photographs on this page show the only major civil engineering work on the Snaefell line at Lhergy Veg where the line had to be carried on a stone-built retaining wall. Following settlement in 1905 the buttresses seen in the photographs were built during the following winter. It has to be said that the weight of these abutments has caused them to settle differentially from the wall that they are supposed to support! Problems continue with settlement between Lhergy Veg and the summit which require constant vigilance and attention during the winter months when the service does not run. The photographs were taken from the opposite side of the valley and clearly show the gradient of the line which is just about on the limit of adhesion without using a rack and pinion system.

We have seen Snaefell cars earlier travelling to Derby Castle depot for painting or major repair. Here is how the Snaefell cars which run on a wider gauge are placed on 3ft gauge trucks for the journey. The Snaefell car is brought down to Laxey Station and placed over a section of dual-gauge track. The car is then jacked up to allow removal of the mountain bogies, the narrower gauge trucks for the MER coastal line are put in place with a bit of sweat and tears and hey presto! This is car *No.3* coming back to Laxey and having the temporary trucks removed.

The power bogies having been brought down from the Snaefell depot are then manually moved into position and fitted to the car. Once both the mountain trucks are in position and connected up the car is propelled, after a bit of judicious shunting, to the depot for the bow collectors to be fitted and final electrical connections made (see page 76). This move of car *No.3* in 1995 would be the last to be carried out in this manner as all future work would be done in the new depot building.

Car *No.5* waits for car *No.2* at the summit. before repositioning on the head spur. Here the differences between it and the other cars after its rebuild can be seen more easily;. the most obvious is the absence of the clerestory light on the roof line and the modern "bus type" windows without the external protective bars. It is popular for corporate entertaining and has a large headlamp fitted for night-time working.

Car *No.2* is now in the head shunt and something has caught the eye of Asst. Operations Manager Paul Ogden. The car is sitting outside the Summit Hotel as rebuilt in 1984 following a fire in the earlier building in 1982. Although still referred to as a hotel it does not have overnight accommodation.

Centenary Year, celebrations are in full swing and the mountain cars had never looked so well. We have seen car *No.3* returning to the mountain after a repaint and it too now has a roof mounted headlamp. During periods that the *Caledonia* was running trips on the mountain, cars were subject to single line working. The third rail fitted for the steam operation can be seen on the up track. It is from this point to the summit that the overhead wiring is dropped in the winter months to avoid wind and ice damage. Asst. Operations Manager Paul Ogden (below) in jovial mood plays host at the summit on Centenary Day.

The sun doesn't always shine at the summit as can be seen in these two photographs but the summer service on the mountain continues regardless offering the visitor the view of the seven kingdoms - Ireland, Scotland, England, Wales, Mann, the Sea and the Kingdom of Heaven. Well, you certainly wouldn't see the latter on a day like this! Spare a thought for the Summit Station Master who has to operate the points and despatch the trams. It didn't matter what the weather was like for the enthusiasts when steam operated on the mountain - they were treated to an unforgettable experience and probably never noticed the view from the western flank over the Sulby reservoir. Nobody in following car **No.6** is looking that way anyway!

Car **No.3** minus its knifeboard advertising panel descends around the north-west shoulder of Snaefell which gave problems to *Caledonia* initially. The views open over the northern plain and on a clear day towards Scotland.

Car **No.3** returning to the depot at Laxey. Although fitted with the rheostatic braking system the calliper brakes are still retained for emergency use and can be clearly seen on this photograph where the depot approach has no Fell centre rail.

An injection of much-needed capital probably helped by the requirements of Health and Safety legislation saw a major refurbishment of Derby Castle depot. New sheds were constructed to modern standards with better lighting and facilities. A new track fan was laid to connect the sheds to the running track.

Snaefell Mountain Railway *No.7* "*Maria*" was brought into Douglas and virtually rebuilt for the Centenary `celebrations of the Snaefell line. The spaciousness of the new sheds is clear in this photograph.

Car **No.6** in the Snaefell depot siding,. on 30th April 1963, is ready to pick up the small goods wagon used to take supplies to the summit. The other is car **No.7** "**Maria**" which was the tram used to take coal to the power station near the Bungalow, borrowing trucks and equipment from one of the other cars as required.

Car **No.7** as fully restored and sitting in the new Laxey depot of the Snaefell Mountain Railway. Such a lot was achieved on the back of the Centenary celebrations of the electric tramways which will stand them in good stead for the future.

The Civil Aviation Authority maintain a radio transmitting station on the summit of Snaefell and because the Snaefell Mountain Railway doesn't run to the summit in the winter they have their own service vehicles which were all supplied by D. Wickham Ltd. The photograph (above) was taken in December 1963. The small vehicle on the left was originally acquired by the Air Ministry in 1951 and still had its original petrol engine at this time. The other vehicle dated from 1958 and was powered by a Ford 28hp diesel engine. The photograph (below) shows the latest vehicle supplied in 1991 and weighing 4 tons unladen is almost twice the weight of the earlier models; it can carry eight people as well as supplies. It is powered by a 4.2 litre Perkins diesel engine.

If you fancy a bracing job in the fresh air then this is for you. Spare a thought for these chaps carrying out repairs to the centre Fell braking rail near the Bungalow in winter-time.

I did say earlier that the Snaefell cars didn't run up the mountain in winter and that wasn't entirely true. Maintenance work has to be done from time to time which involves running beyond the Bungalow but the summit is not accessible by the electric cars until the overhead is put back on the last section. If Easter is early then that work may have to be carried out in inclement weather.

The opening ceremony to celebrate the Centenary of the Manx Electric Railway. the Hon. Alan Bell M.H.K, then the Minister of the Department of Tourism and Leisure under whose auspices National Transport falls, addressed the assembled crowd on 10th April 1993 prior to inviting the Governor Air Marshal Sir Laurence Jones, KCB, AFC to drive car *No.1* through the opening tape to get the proceedings under way.

1993 was designated "The Year of Railways" and in August during centenary fortnight of the MER a spectacular cavalcade of trams was held at Laxey when every serviceable tram paraded through the station. Maurice Faragher gave a comprehensive commentary describing each tram as it passed at what became one of the highlights of the year. Car *No.1* is about to break the tape which is being held by Robert Smith, nearest the camera, then the Chief Executive of National Transport, and start the parade.

The Centenary celebrations were brilliant and full of special events. IMR **No.4 Loch** was at Laxey to represent the steam railway involvement in the extension from Laxey to Ramsey when IMR **No.2 Derby**, which no longer exists, was used by the contractor building the line. I suppose any excuse was better than none and it too produced some unforgettable scenes. **No.4** is photographed crossing the Ramsey Road on its return from one of the runs to the Dhoon.

1995 was the Centenary of the Snaefell Mountain Railway and flushed with the success two years earlier was designated "International Year of the Railways". It saw IMR **No.15 Caledonia** also running steam trips on the MER between Laxey and the Dhoon. It is seen in the photograph passing Dhoon Halt.

Again using the same theme as the involvement of IMR *No.4* in the MER Centenary, the highlight without any doubt for the Snaefell Centenary was the resurrection of IMR *No.15 Caledonia* from the Port Erin Museum and its restoration to full working condition to commemorate it's use by the contractor who built the Snaefell Mountain Railway. Here are more pictures from the trials undertaken earlier in the year to satisfy the Railway Inspector. It's another of those bracing open air jobs that people who don't have to do them hanker for!

The six cars in the Snaefell Mountain railway fleet assembled at the summit on centenary day presenting a rare photo opportunity for enthusiasts and the general public alike. In complete contrast to the weather seen on some of the earlier photographs the weather on the day was superb.

Another cavalcade of trams, this time lined up at Lag Birragh and ready for a run back to Derby Castle for night-time photography at the depot. It was yet another of the events laid on for the general public and visiting enthusiasts who came from all over the world for the fortnight.

"Steam 125" in 1998 was the last really big enthusiasts event to be organised and the reason was to celebrate one hundred-and-twenty-five years of the steam railway's existence. IMR **No.1 Sutherland** was brought out of the Port Erin Museum and restored to full running order for the event. "What has that got to do with trams" I hear you ask? Well, here is the reason. To dream up yet another novelty event the MER effectively said you have had steam on the electric railways, how about electric on the steam railway! Car **No.33** was chosen and a generator van constructed to provide the power, and once again - hey presto! The upper photograph shows the tram on one of its evaluation trials in January 1998 prior to inspection by the Railway Inspector, with Colin Goldsmith riding shotgun. The result (below) was that enthusiasts, for a fee, could enjoy the novelty of a ride on the steam railway in an open tramcar and really see the line as never before.

Steam was back at Laxey during Enthusiasts Week in 1998, when enthusiasts from all over the world were on the Isle of Man to witness three **No.1s** on the MER and what a glorious sight it was. They could travel behind steam on the MER again but this time to the south of Laxey from Laxey Station to Fairy Cottage and accompanied by a photographers tram on the adjacent track.

I mentioned earlier the late Mike Goodwin and his involvement with Keith Pearson and myself in "Tramways of the Isle of Man". What I didn't mention was that he later went on to work for the Manx Electric Railway as a driver. In this photograph, included as a tribute to him, he is driving car **No.2** during one of the special celebratory events when the two original cars were running side by side from Derby Castle to Groudle.

A tail-end view to finish on, from the parade along King Edward Road during the International Year of the Railways. A conductor's eye view of car *No.2* from car *No.1*, both dating from 1893 and the oldest working tramcars in the world - treasure them!